# Books, Books, Books

## A Treasury of Clip Art

Darcie Clark Frohardt

1995

**Libraries Unlimited, Inc.**

**Englewood, Colorado**

LIBRARIES UNLIMITED, INC.
P.O. Box 6633
Englewood, CO 80155-6633
1-800-237-6124

**Library of Congress Cataloging-in-Publication Data**

Frohardt, Darcie Clark.
    Books, books, books : a treasury of clip art / Darcie Clark
Frohardt.
    vi, 104 p.  22x28 cm.
    Includes index.
    ISBN 1-56308-265-9
    1. Clip art.  I. Title.
Z250.3.F76  1995
741.6--dc20                                    94-30829
                                                   CIP

# Contents

# Introduction

The purpose of clip art is to assist in the creation of printed products: flyers, posters, newsletters, bulletin boards, announcements, award certificates, bookmarks—the uses are endless! In examining other books of clip art the author found much that applied to general topics, such as holiday pictures, pictures of children, and contemporary topics, but little that applied to books—children with books, animal characters with books, holiday themes incorporating books, and the like. This book of 392 original images is designed for librarians, teachers, storytellers, and other people interested in using illustrations themed around books.

All the clip art in this book can be copied, photographed, traced, or otherwise modified for use in printed products. If you are producing a publication that will be sold, such as a history of your local library, you may also use this clip art. Only if you are producing a book of designs for sale, such as a coloring book or other book of clip art, must permission be sought from the publisher. (Reselling these pictures as clip art in print or electronic form is, of course, prohibited.)

The clip art is divided into seven sections. Each section contains both silhouettes and line drawings that will reproduce well, even on a photocopier. "Just Books" includes books on shelves and in piles, stacked books, animated book characters, and open books. "People with Books" presents people in all types of situations involving books (e.g., the aged, young, sitting, in groups). "Nursery Rhymes and Characters" has all the favorites! Jack Sprat, Old Mother Hubbard, Humpty Dumpty, Mary Poppins, Cinderella, and more. "Animals" includes an elephant, fish, dogs, cats, horses, and that perennial favorite, dinosaurs—all with books. "Holidays" will spice up activities with themes from Cinco de Mayo, July 4th, Mother's and Father's Day, Christmas, Hanukkah, Earth Day, and so on; it also includes seasonal icons and themes. "Sports and Activities" amuses with Olympic events, dancing, and all the major sports. Finally, "Borders" provides a wide variety of unique borders incorporating elements from the other chapters.

## How to Use This Book

Some basic supplies are needed to effectively create printed materials. Gather together the following supplies and be set to go: a metal ruler, T-square, and triangle to keep everything straight; "X-Acto" ® knife and blades for cutting in small spaces; a light blue nonreproducible pencil or pen for marking lines (this pencil will not photograph and does not show when the project is printed or photocopied); rubber cement; an art gum eraser; pens and markers; masking tape to secure your artwork to a working surface; and a glue stick.

Use eye-catching words in the main headline of your print product. Create a "dummy" of your project using a sheet of paper the size of the finished project. Place graphics and text on this sheet to position the elements correctly. A photocopier works well to enlarge or reduce an image to the desired size. Colored inks or papers are worth their extra expense!

Using a photocopier is the least expensive method for reproducing small quantities of items. To assure a clean, professional look, always use paste in moderation so as not to create lumpy areas. Keep your work area clean and use only permanent ink markers to avoid smearing. If shadow lines appear when an image has been pasted into position, you can use correction fluid to paint out the shadows before you print the final product.

All the visual tools are here for adding a whimsical or serious touch to your printed materials. Have fun with this book—experiment and be creative.

# Just Books

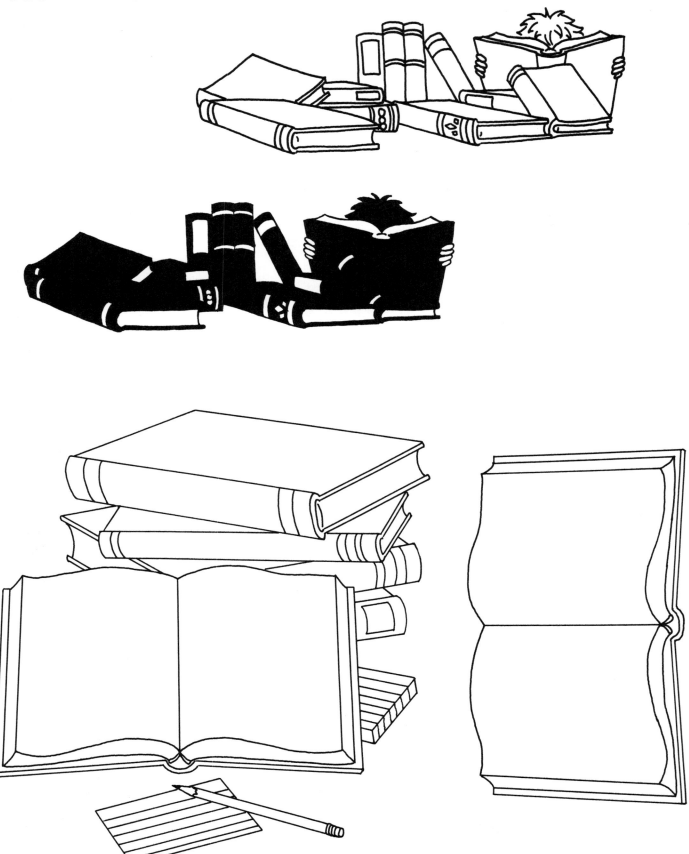

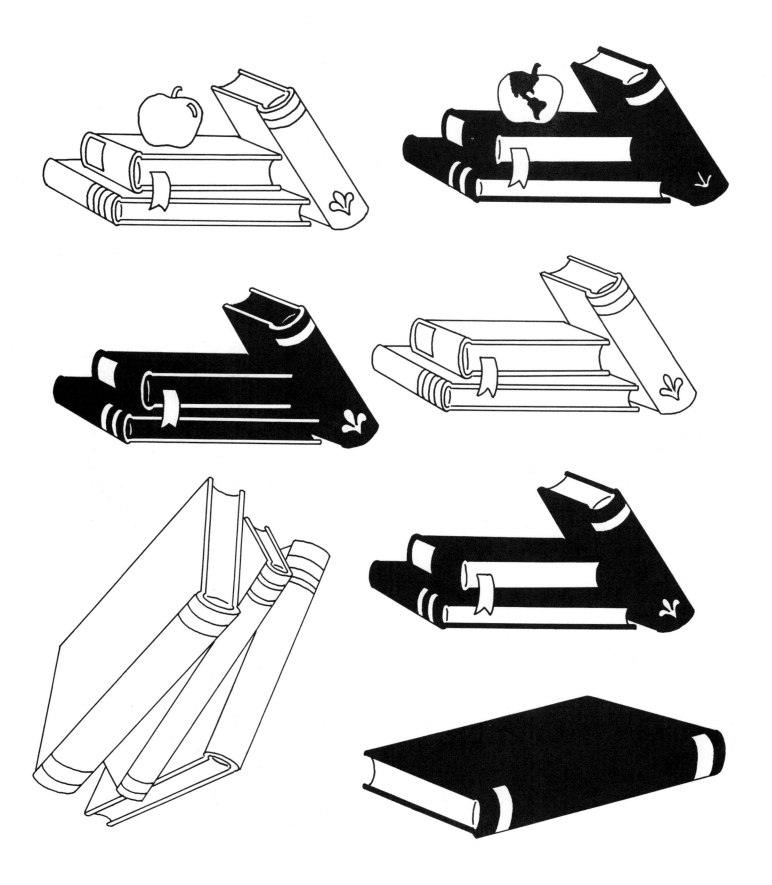

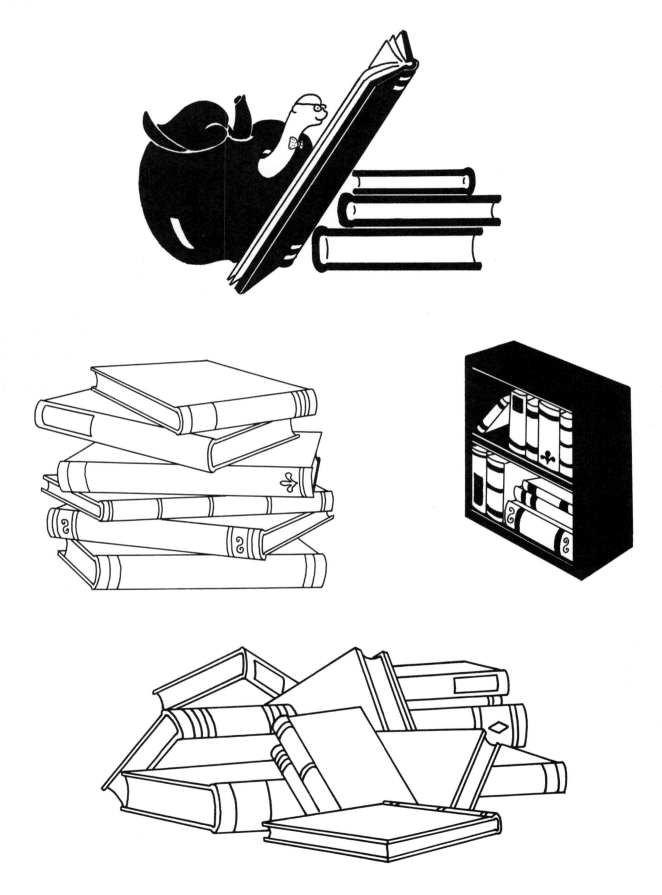

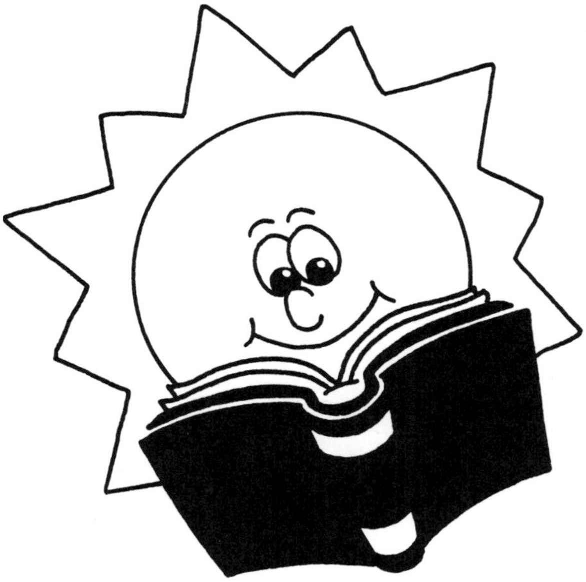

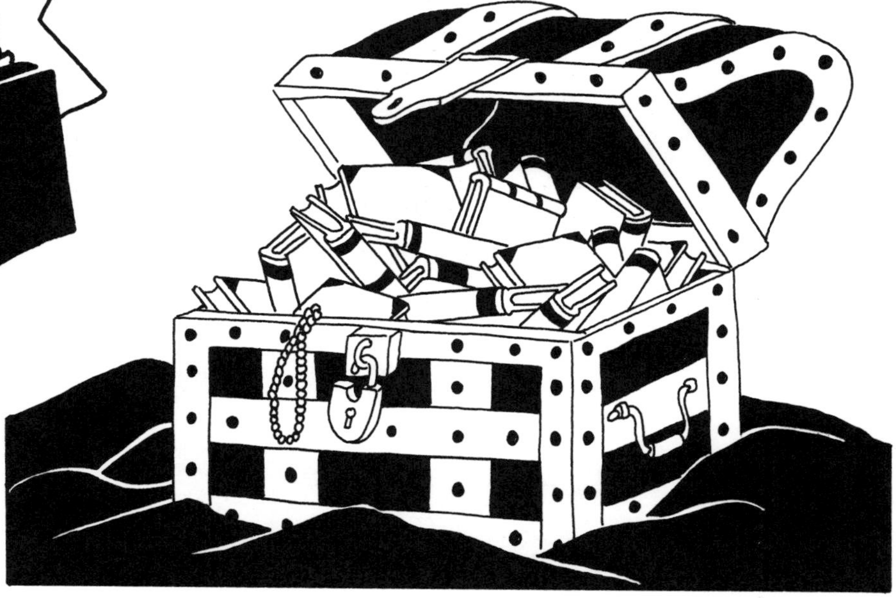

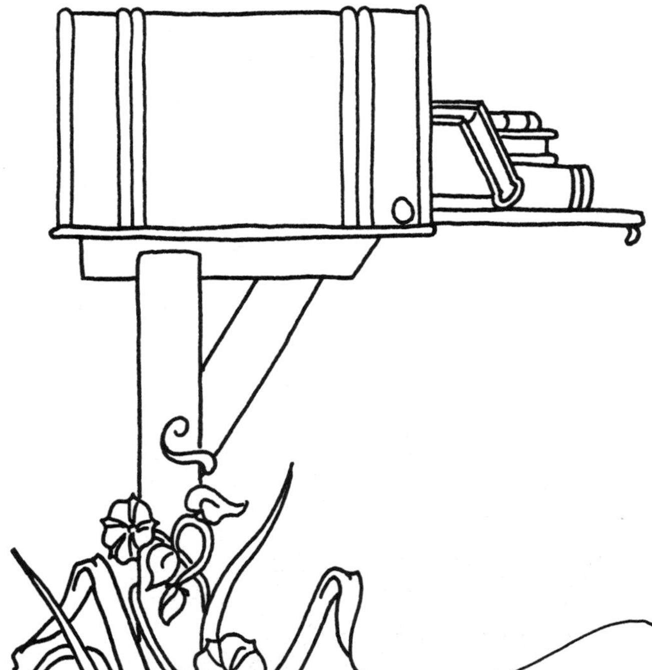

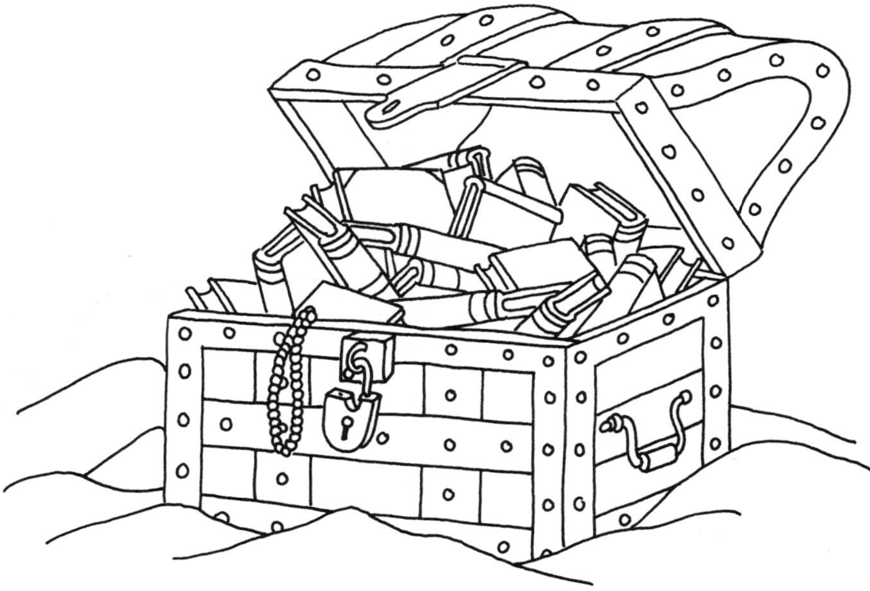

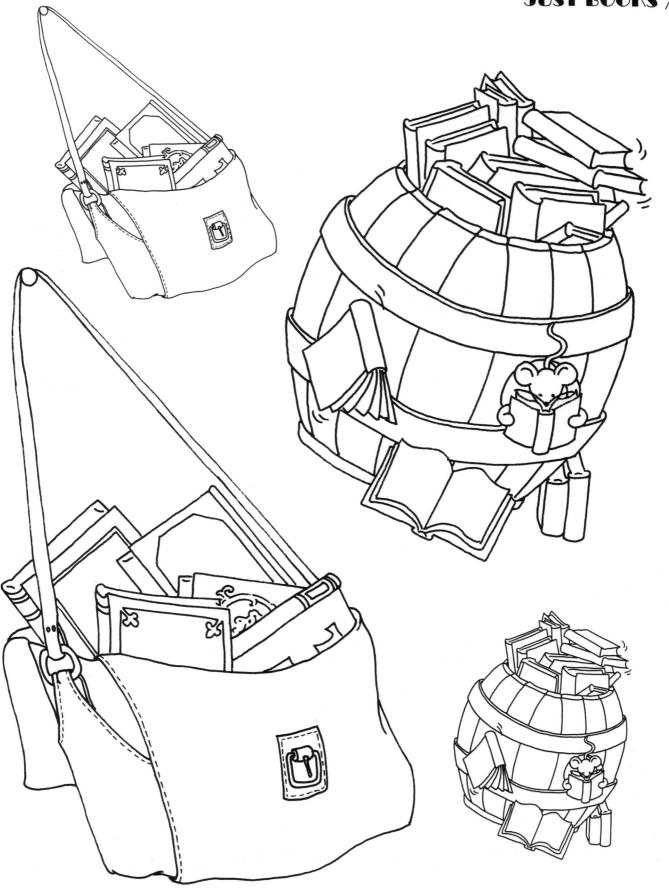

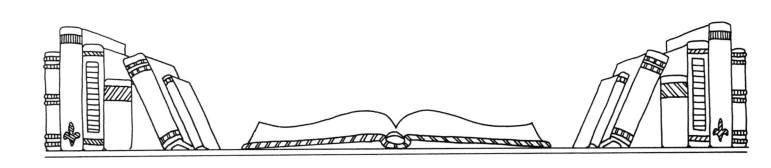

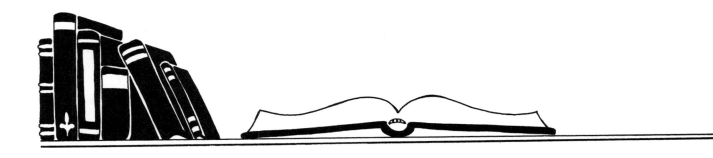

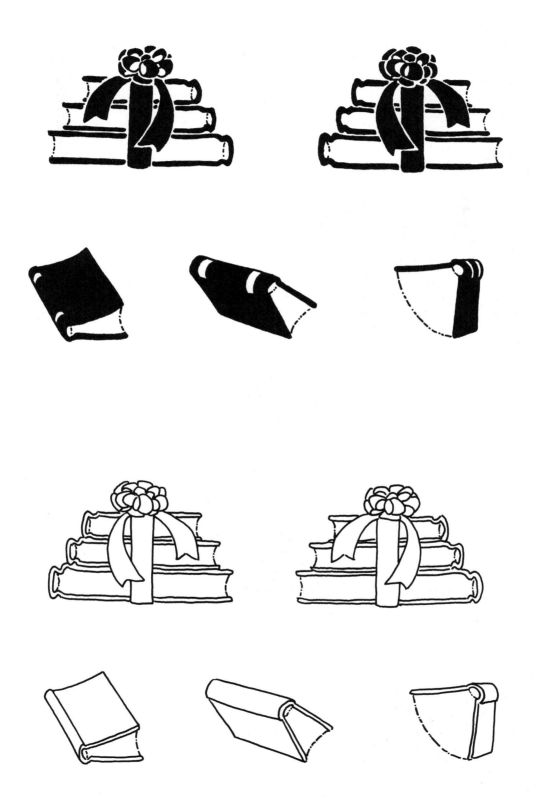

# People with Books

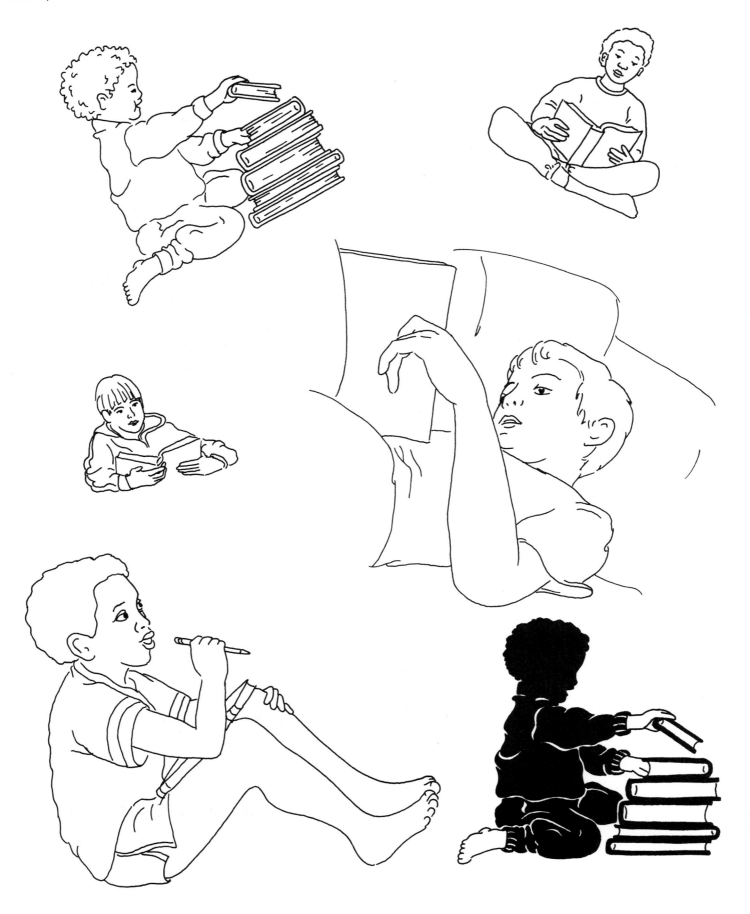

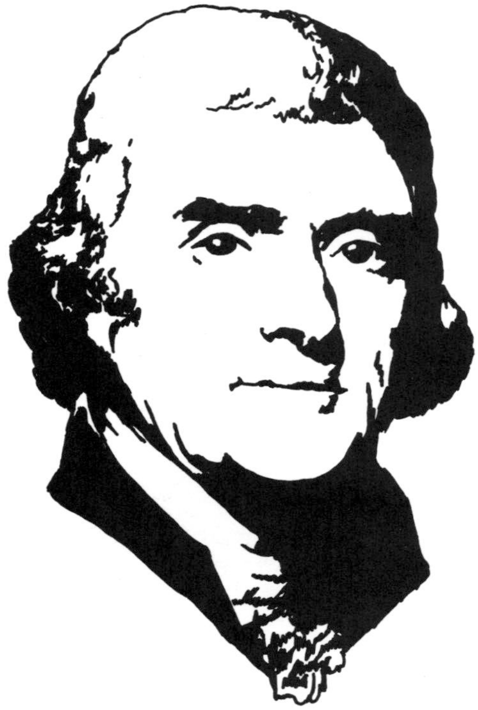

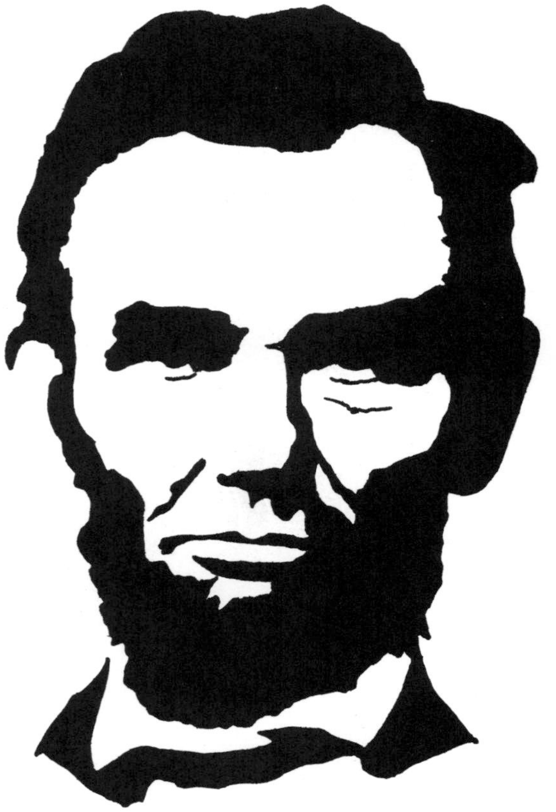

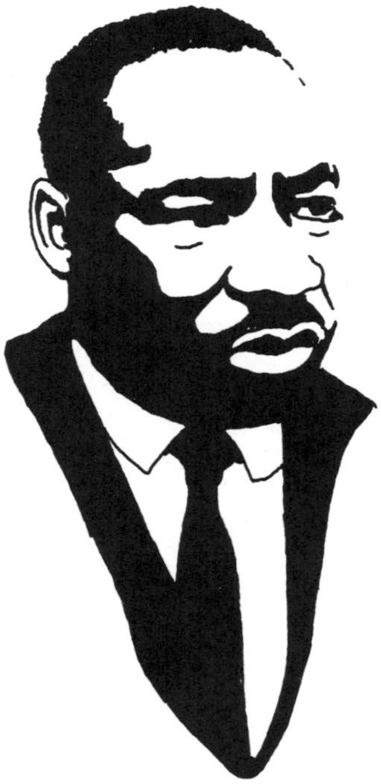

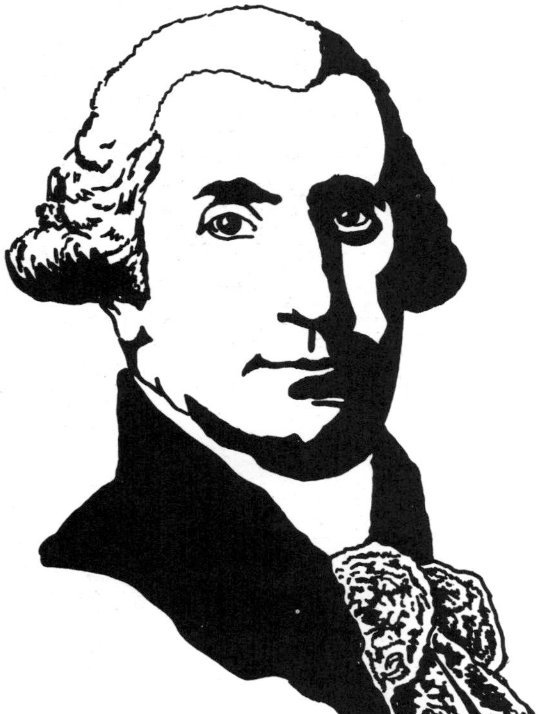

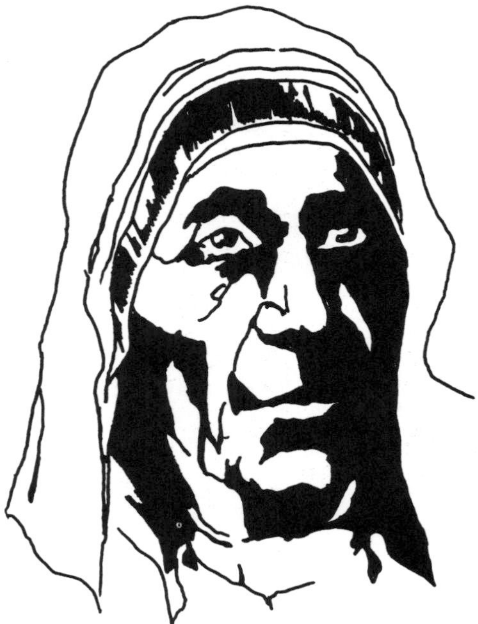

# Animals

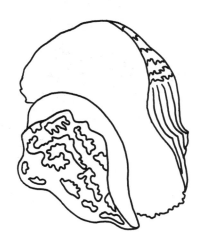

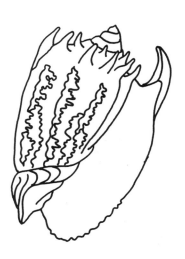

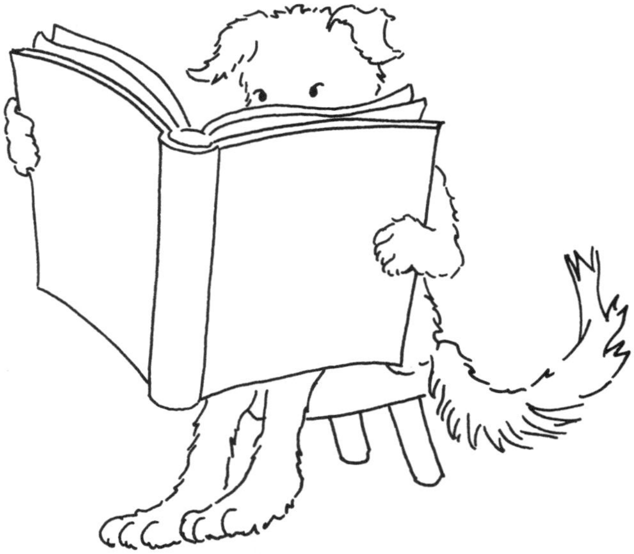

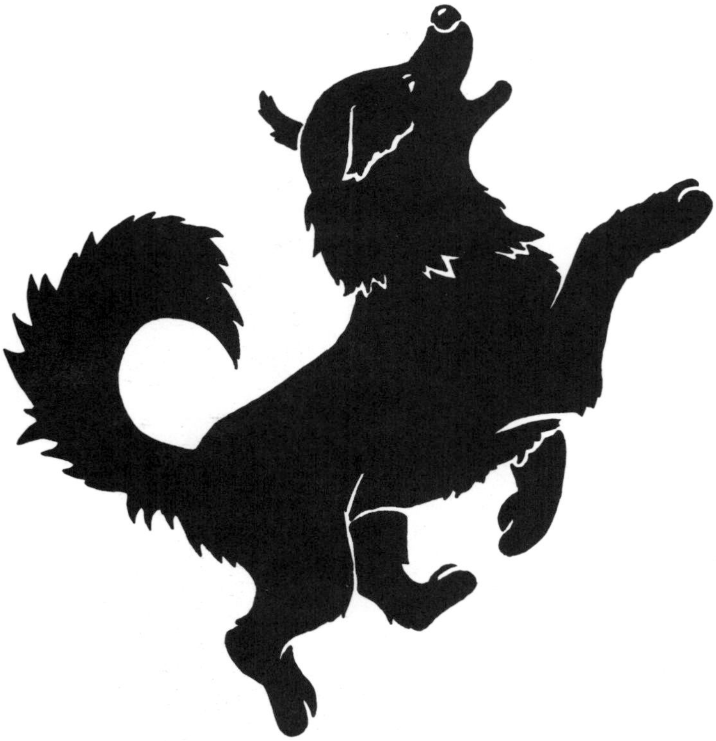

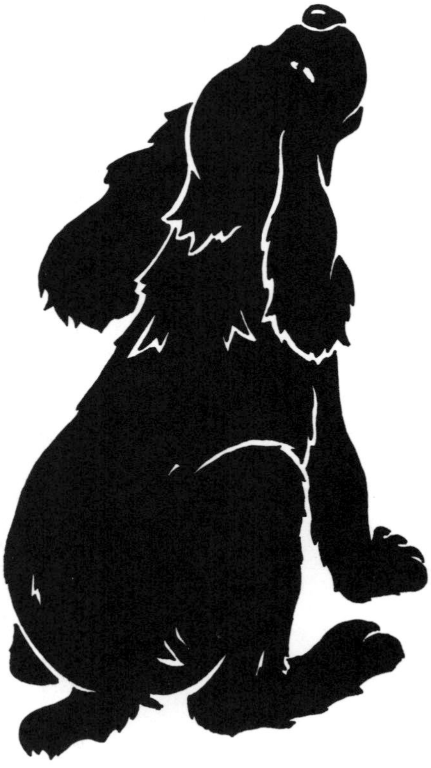

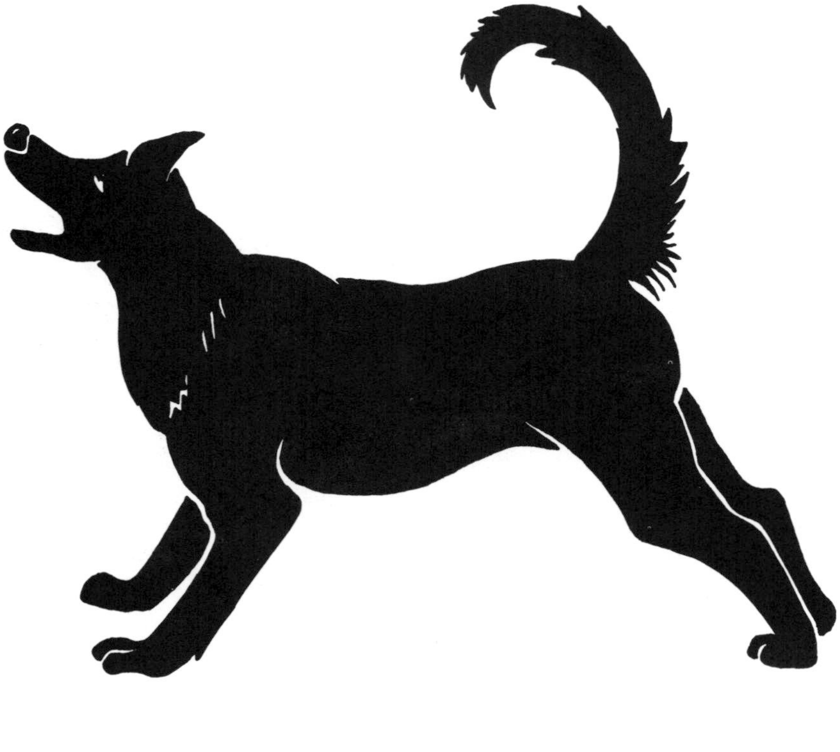

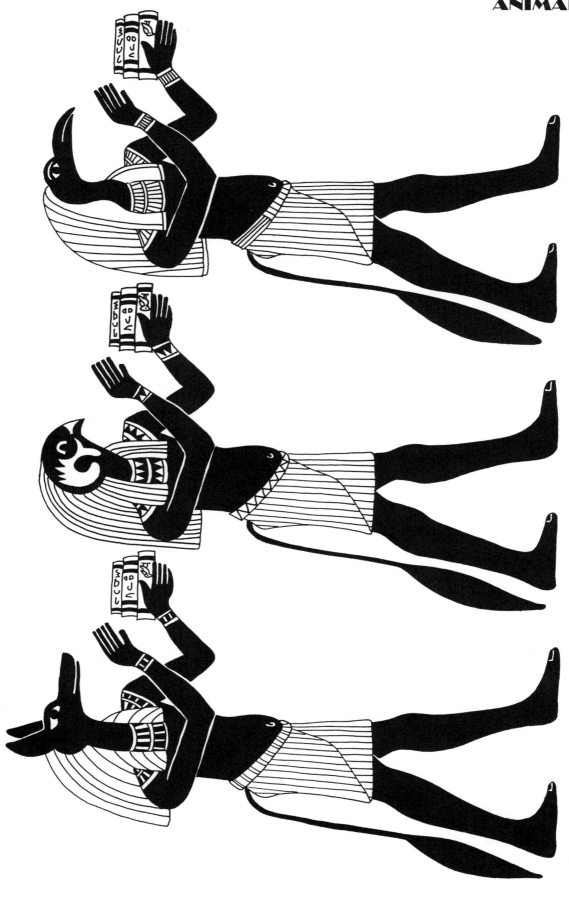

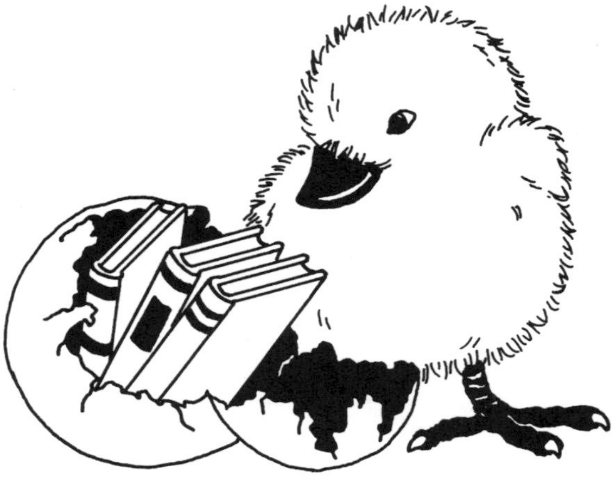

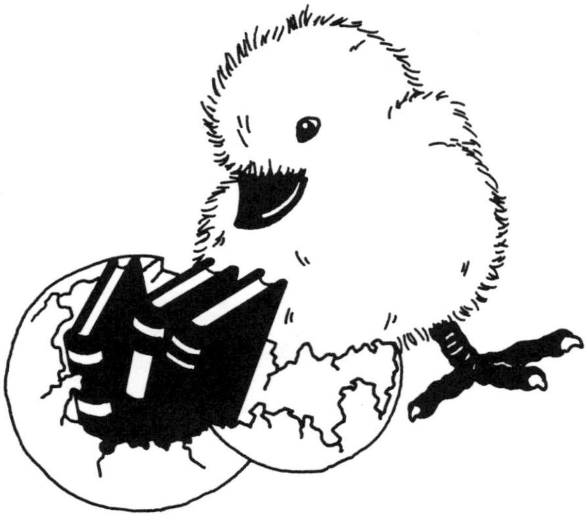

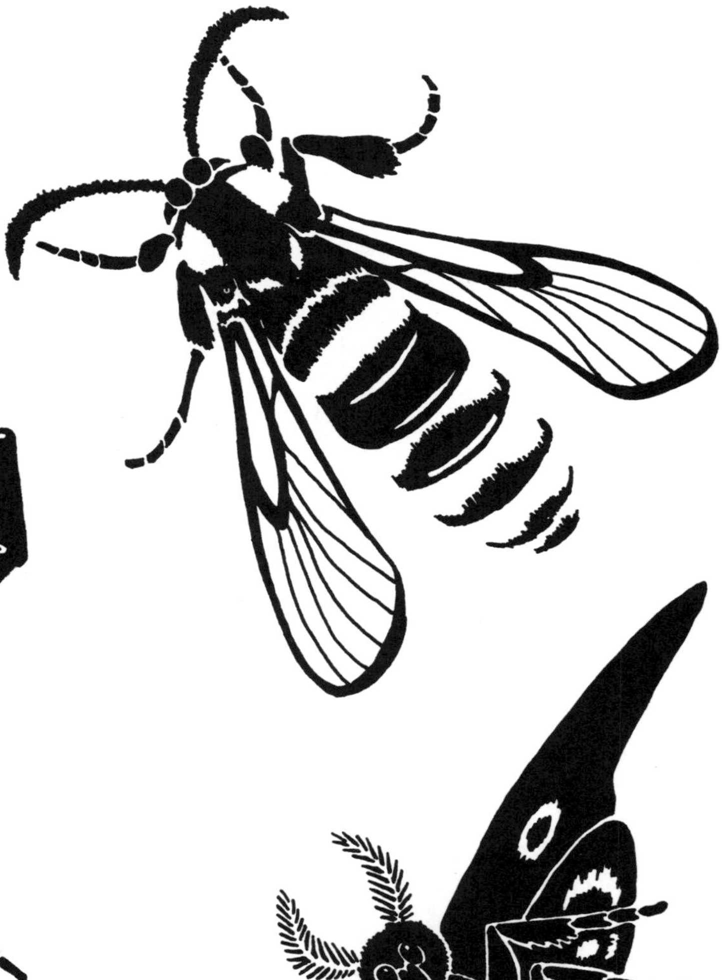

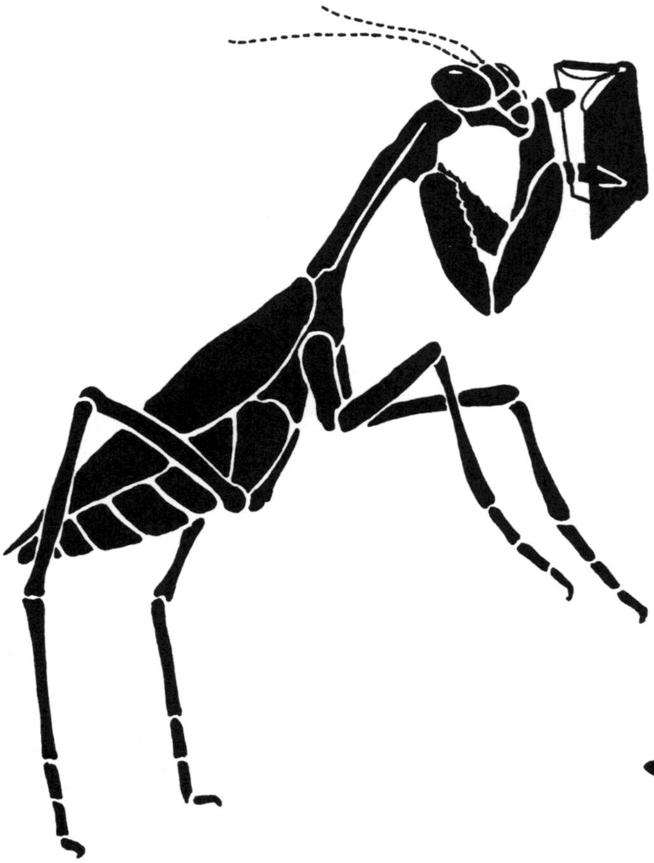

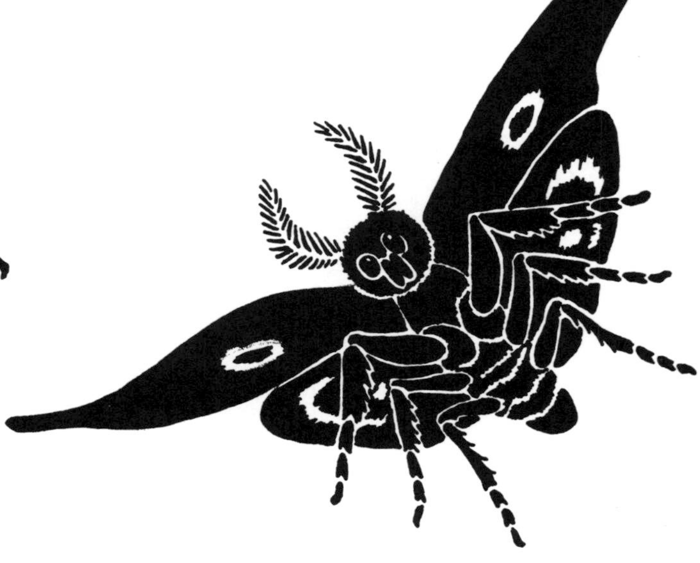

# Nursery Rhymes and Characters

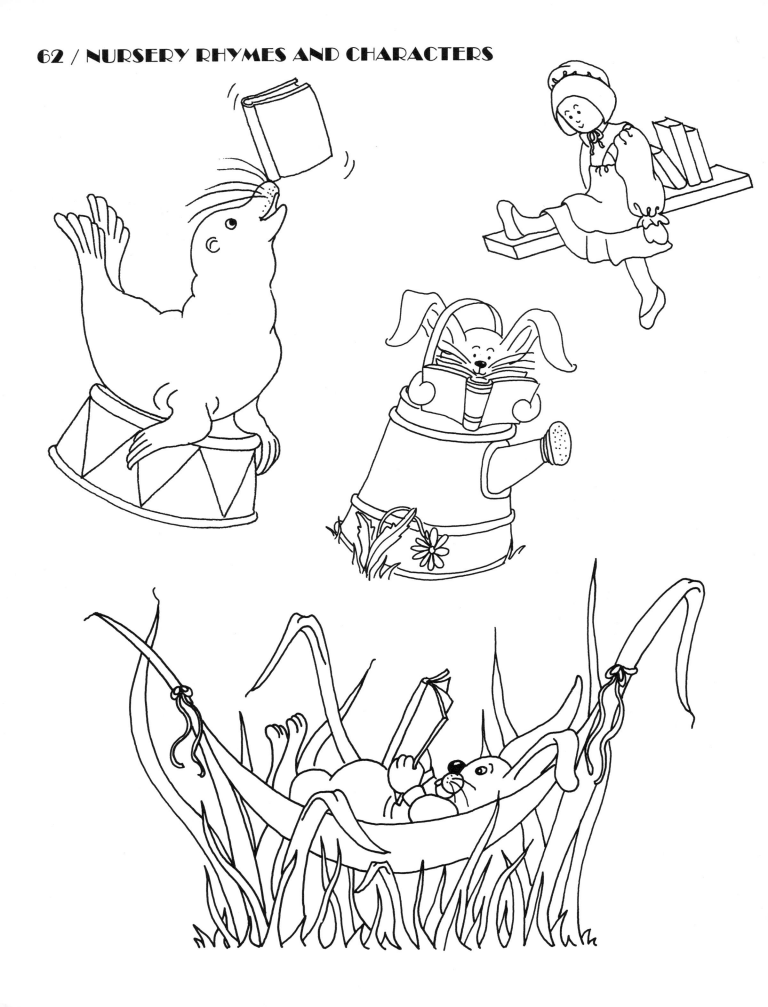

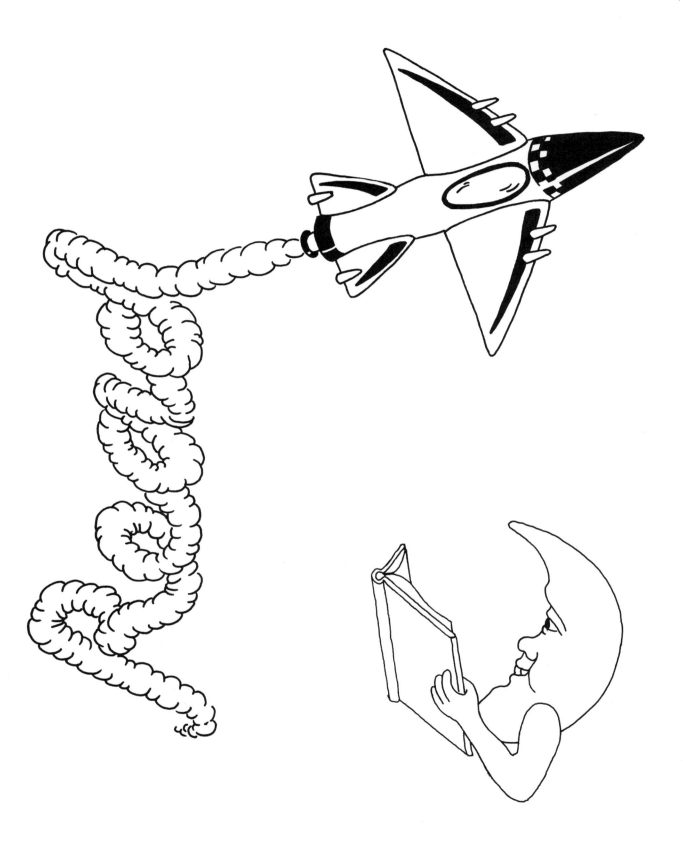

# Holidays

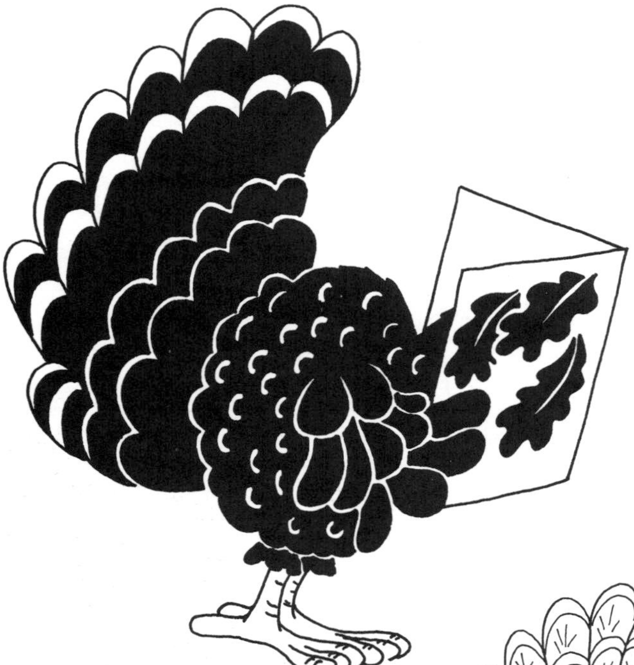

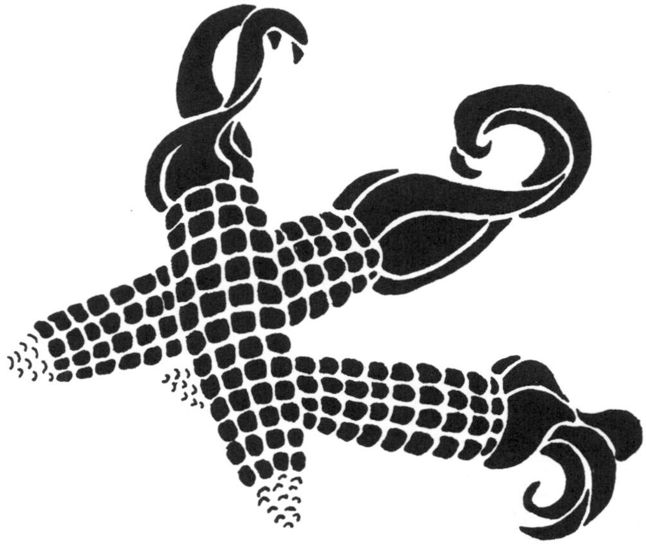

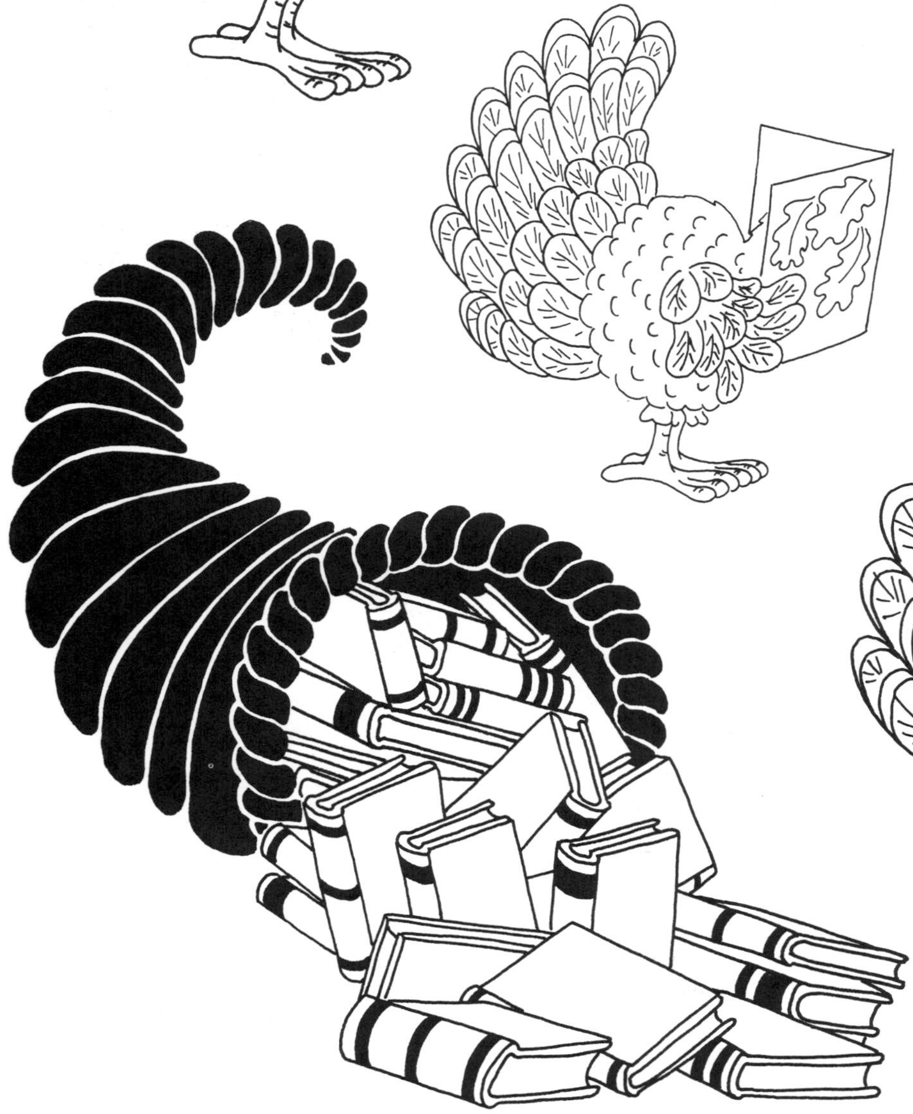

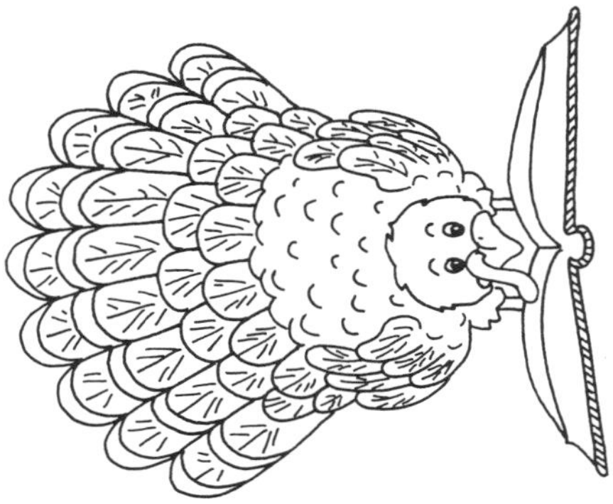

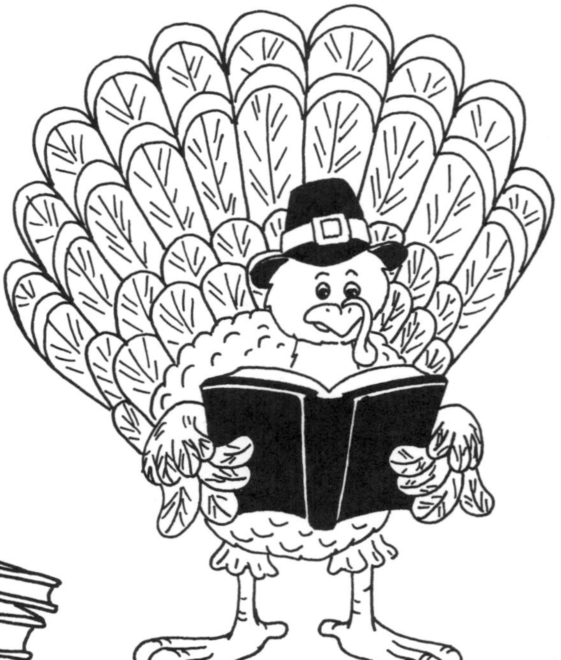

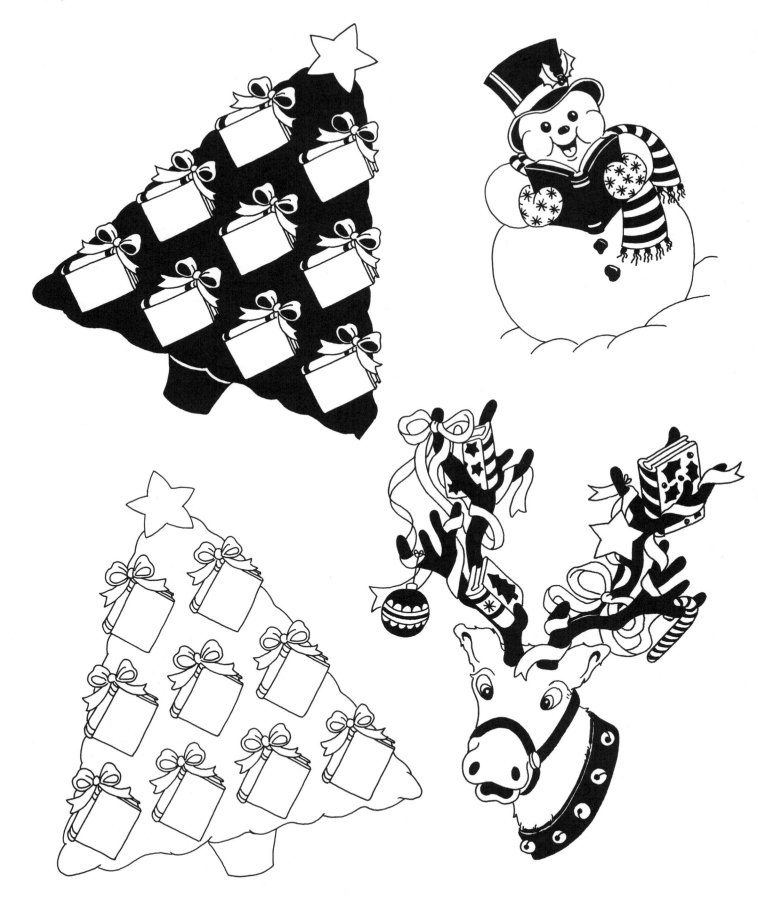

# Sports and Activities

# Borders

This book
belongs to

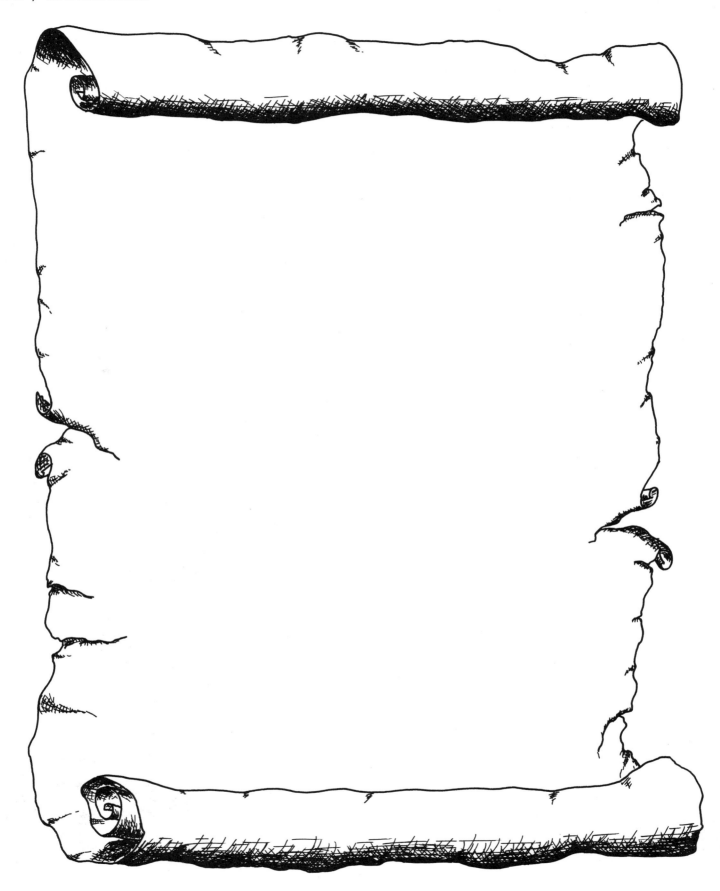

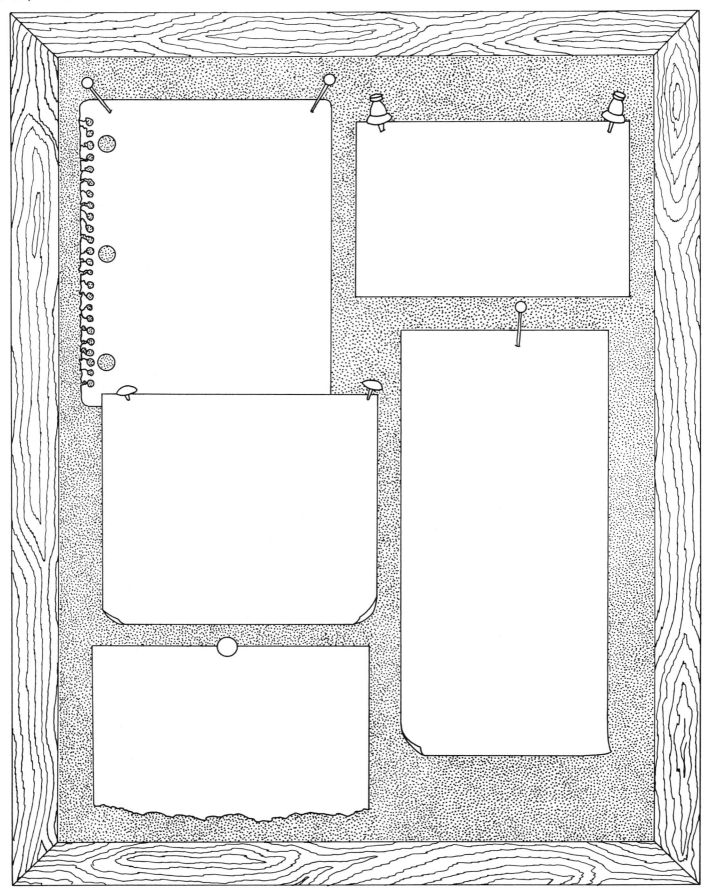

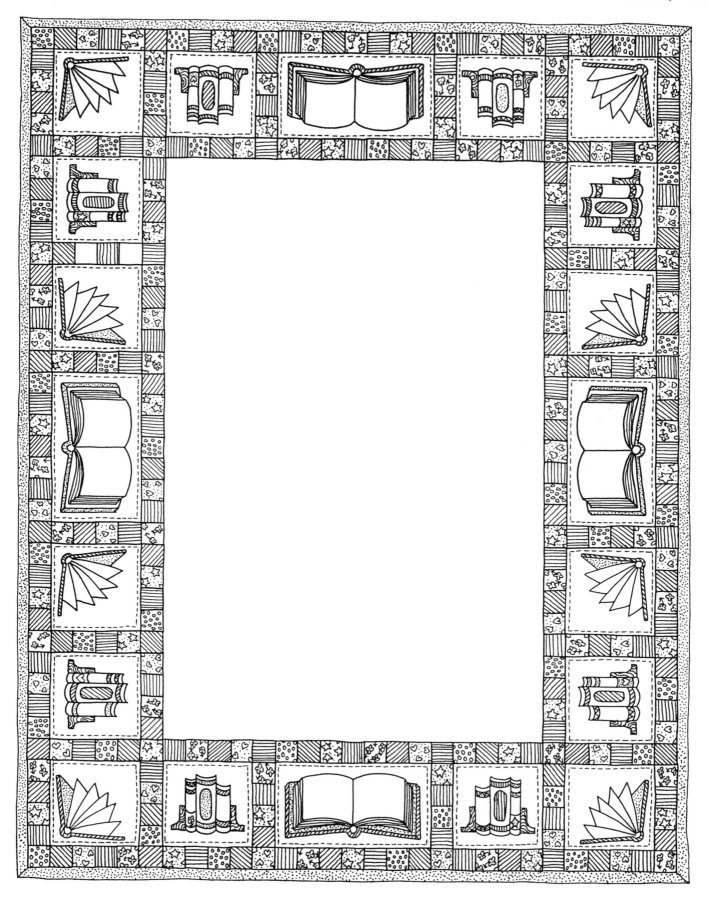

# Index